Rookie Read-About™ Science

How Do You Know It's Spring?

By Allan Fowler

Consultants:
Robert L. Hillerich, Ph.D., Bowling Green
State University, Bowling Green, Ohio

Mary Nalbandian, Director of Science,
Chicago Public Schools, Chicago, Illinois

Fay Robinson, Child Development Specialist

CHILDRENS PRESS®
CHICAGO

Series cover and interior design by Sara Shelton

Library of Congress Cataloging–in–Publication Data

Fowler, Allan.
   How do you know it's spring? / by Allan Fowler.
     p. cm.—(Rookie read-about science)
   Summary: A simple description of the characteristics of spring.
   ISBN 0-516-04914-3
   1. Spring—Juvenile literature. [1. Spring.] I. Title.
II. Series: Fowler, Allan. Rookie read-about science.
QB637.5.F68   1991
508—dc20   91-12760
                                            CIP
                                            AC

How do you know it's spring?

When leaves begin to grow
on the trees...

when the grass turns green
again...

6

when the first flowers
bloom in your garden or
in the park, then you know
it's springtime!

Last fall, the robins flew south where it's warmer.

They spent all winter there.

But now it's spring and the robins are back.

Birds can tell when it's spring, and time to build their nests,

lay their eggs, and hatch
their babies.

Many baby animals are
born in the spring.

You know it's spring when winter's last snows have melted and filled the rivers and streams with rushing water.

Or when you can go outside
without a heavy coat and
still feel warm.

But some days you need an umbrella to stay dry during spring showers.

You know it's spring when
you hear the crack of a
bat hitting a baseball,

when you and your friends
can't wait to ride your bikes,

or put on your roller skates,

or have fun at the playground.

Spring is the time for farmers to plow their fields so they can plant their crops.

It's the time for you to plant seeds if you have a garden.

Easter and Passover come
in the spring.

Mother's Day

and Memorial Day come
in the spring.

Most adults don't get a
spring vacation–but you
do.

So why not go outside
and play?

It's spring!

Words You Know

spring

leaves

grass

eggs in a nest

robin

spring showers

farmer plowing field

grass seeds sprouting

flowers

31

Index

About the Author

Allan Fowler is a free-lance writer with a background in advertising. Born in New York, he lives in Chicago now and enjoys traveling.

Photo Credits

PhotoEdit—© Myrleen Ferguson, 20, 23; © Tony Freeman, 27, 28

Valan—© Pierre Kohler, Cover; © Kennon Cooke, 4, 16; © Karen D. Rooney, 5; © Wouterloot-Gregoire, 6; © Stephen Krasemann, 9, 15; © James M. Richards, 10; © Albert Kuhnigk, 11; © Wayne Lankinen, 12; © D. Schmidt, 13; © Dr. A. Farquhar, 17; © J.R. Page, 18; © Val Whelan, 22; © V. Wilkinson, 24

SuperStock International, Inc.—24; © Tom Rosenthal, 19

© Jim Whitmer—21, 26

COVER: Apple blossoms